Lamoni Call

2000 Changes in the Book of Mormon

Lamoni Call

2000 Changes in the Book of Mormon

ISBN/EAN: 9783337259983

Printed in Europe, USA, Canada, Australia, Japan

Cover: Foto ©Lupo / pixelio.de

More available books at **www.hansebooks.com**

2000
CHANGES IN THE
BOOK OF MORMON.

CONTAINING

The way the book is claimed to have been translated, The amendments which have been made in the book. What an inspired translation should have been, and the reasons given by the church for making the many grammatical changes.

SHOWING

That the claims are inconsistent and untrue.

BY LAMONI CALL,
COMPILER OF "THE GOSPEL IN A NUT SHELL."

BOUNTIFUL, UTAH,
AUG. 1898.

PREFACE.

In lifting my pen against the book my friends hold as sacred, I realize, in part, at least, my position. My friends and relatives are mostly in the church, and many of them look with pity upon my position; while I regard my difference of opinion as purely a mental conviction, and cannot see how any person can injure himself in the sight of God if he does only what he thinks is right. To advise one not to think in any particular way would be as inconsistent as to ask the powers of gravitation not to attract. A person may, however, for aught I know, do something which will cause God to withdraw his spirit from him so that he will not then believe as he once did. But I see no difference as to the cause of one's belief, the only thing for we poor mortals is to do as we think we should do. We cannot even follow the convictions of yesterday, nor can we follow those we may have to-morrow. The thing to do is to do what we believe we should do now. Emerson has in his essay on "Self-reliance" (I should like to incorporate the entire essay as part of this preface.) "If you would be a man, speak what you think to-day in words as hard as cannon balls, and to-morrow speak what to-morrow thinks in hard words again; though it contradict everything you said to-day." A person might be held accountable for doing the thing that caused his mind to change; if it be a crime, he would be held accountable whether his mind changed or not; if honest investigation, that is a praiseworthy-act at any time, and our investigations should be made without fear of being convinced in any particular way.

Since, then, I do not believe the Book of Mormon is a gift of heaven to man, there are but three reasons why I should not raise my voice and pen to proclaim against it. One of these is the lack of ability. Another is the lack of energy. The other is the lack of courage. The last two have not stood in the way, but I am not so sure but many will say the first should.

What makes me the more anxious to write my views is because I have been unable to satisfy myself that my stand is wrong, and no person with whom I have been able to converse upon the subject has been able to show me the fallacy in my argument. It may exist for all that, and there may be plenty of people able to help me. The publication of this little work will put them in possession of one of my difficulties, which if they can remove, will give me great hope that the others' may be removed. If truth is against me I most sincerely hope some person with the spirit of sympathy burning deep in his bosom will step forward and save another soul unto Christ. Be assured, if you come with REASON you will be considered, but do not ask me to lay aside my mind and take that of any other person.

I have endeavored to write without animosity, and to use nothing of a repulsive nature. No vile names are used. But in all cases reference is made to matters of history in the most respectful language at my command. I believe those who hold the Book of Mormon as sacred can read without having their ire aroused by false statements, or abusive accusations.

THE AUTHOR.

How the Plates Were Translated.

IT MAY not seem a matter of importance to some to learn just how the plates were translated. But it seems to me that a great matter rests upon even this small point of history.

If it is a fact that Joseph had the plates as he said, and translated them as we are told he did, the probabilities are that those who were intimately connected with the work would get a correct understanding of the way it was done, and we would be furnished with correct data regarding so great a subject.

I have considered, carefully, all the references made to the way the work of translation was performed that I have been able to find, but at present cannot tell how the work was accomplished.

It is necessary that we learn as much about the historical evidence as we can before we enter into the subject matter of this little work. Indeed we should have the whole truth to do it justice. But since I have not found what satisfies me as being the whole truth, we will go to work as best we can.

Elder George Reynolds, in writing on the subject of "Time Occupied in Translating the Book of Mormon," says:

1. "Objection has been made to the divinity of the Book of Mormon on the ground that the account given in the publications of the Church, of the time occupied in the work of translation is far too short for the accomplishment of such a labor, and consequently it must have been copied or transcribed from some work written in the English language, most probably from Spaulding's 'Manuscript Found.' But at the outset it must be recollected that the translation was accomplished by no common method, by

no ordinary means. It was done by divine aid. There were no delays over obscure passages, no difficulties over the choice of words, no stoppages from the ignorance of the translator; no time was wasted in investigation or argument over the value, intent or meaning of certain characters, and there were no references to authorities. These difficulties to human work were removed. All was as simple as when a clerk writes from dictation. The translation of the characters appeared on the Urim and Thummim, sentence by sentence, and as soon as one was correctly transcribed the next would appear. So the enqiry narrows down to the consideration of this simple question, how much could Oliver Cowdrey write in a day?"—Myth of the Manuscript Found, Page 71.

Again, from the same author, we have a quotation from Martin Harris, one of the three witnesses, Joseph's first scribe, a man who befriended Joseph, and was in his company at first, when the work was yet in embryo; the man who saw as much of the process as God designed man—other than his prophet Joseph—to see at that time:

2. "He said that the Prophet possessed a seer

stone, by which he was enabled to translate as well as from the Urim and Thummim, and for convenience he then used the seer stone. Martin explained the translation as follows: By aid of the seer stone, sentences would appear and were read by the prophet and written by Martin, and when finished he would say, 'Written,' and if correctly written, that sentence would disappear and another appear in its place, but if not written correctly it remained until corrected, so that the translation was just as it was engraven on the plates, precisely in the language then used."—Myth of the Manuscript Found, Page 91.

M. T. Lamb has quoted David Whitmer's description of the process from the Deseret Evening News of December 24, 1885:

3. "After affixing the magical spectacles to his eyes, Smith would take the plates and translate the characters one at a time. The graven characters would appear in succession to the seer, and directly under the character, when viewed through the glasses, would be the translation in English."—The Golden Bible, page 241.

B. H. Roberts, in his "Brief History of the Church," has the following footnote, but he does not tell where he gets it. O. F. Whitney has almost the same thing in his "History of Utah;"

4. "The following is the manner in which it is said the Book of Mormon was translated: 'The Prophet, scanning through the Urim and Thummim the golden pages, would see appear, in lieu of the strange characters engraved thereon, their equivalent in English words. These he would repeat, and the scribe, separated from him by a veil or curtain, would write them down, * * * Until the writing was correct in every particular, the words last given would remain before the eyes of the translator, and not disappear. But on the necessary correction being made, they would immediately pass away and be succeeded by others.' "—Brief History of the Church, page 28.

Dr. Wyle, an anti-Mormon author, quotes Emma's—the Prophet's first wife—death-bed statement to her son Joseph:

5. "In writing for your father I frequently wrote day after day, often sitting at the table close by him, he sitting with his face buried in his hat with the stone in it."—Mormon Portraits, page 203.

Daniel P. Kidder published a work in 1842. This, too, is anti-Mormon, and we can take it for what it is worth. We make an extract from a statement made by Joseph's father-in-law, Isaac Hale:

6. "The manner in which he pretended to read and interpret, was the same as when he looked for the money-diggers, with the stone in his hat, and his hat over his face, while the book of plates was at the same time hid in the woods."—Mormonism and the Mormons, page 32.

A Chicago Times correspondent visited David Whitmer, and published an article which was criticised by the Deseret Evening News at the time. Our extract was not criticised, so it must have been correct, according to the ideas of the editor:

7. "Frequently one character would make two lines of manuscript, while others made but a word or two words."—Myth of M. F., page 83.

In order to avoid trouble in calling

attention to the above extracts we have numbered them.

The only point of interest to me in Nos. 5 and 6 is that the stone was placed in Joseph's hat. Just where the plates were I cannot tell, for if Joseph had the stone and his face buried in his hat, it is hardly probable that the plates could have been there too. If they were, the light must have peen excluded, so he could not view them with his natural eyes, and the work could not be read as we would read a work by the light of the sun.

Extract No. one says: "The translation of the characters appeared ON the Urim and Thummim." No. three says Joseph viewed the characters "THROUGH" the glasses. No. four also says that he viewed the plates THROUGH the Urim and Thummim. The question which now presents itself is, did the translation appear ON the stone, or

Urim and Thummim, or did Joseph look THROUGH the instrument and see the translation beyond it, or was it sometimes one way and sometimes the other way. As a matter of fact, after reading what all three extracts say, I do not know anything about it.

Number three says: "The graven characters would appear in succession to the seer, and directly under the character, when viewed through the glasses, would be the translation in English. In number four Joseph "would see appear, IN LIEU of the strange characters engraven thereon, their equivalent in English words." Number one says "The translation of the characters appeared on the Urim and Thummim." It is important that we understand this matter, so please note carefully. Number three says both character and English appeared, number four says only the English appeared; number one says the translation appeared, but says nothing about the characters appearing. So after getting all I can out of this, I am not certain of the way the translation was performed.

Number seven may throw a little light on the subject: "Frequently one character would make two lines of manuscript, while others would make but a word or two words." If the English appeared IN LIEU of the characters, how could Joseph tell which character made the English before him? And if the translation only came up upon the Urim and Thummim, how could he tell what part of the record he was working on? How could he tell when to turn over the leaf? Or is it a fact that they sometimes translated with the plates in the woods? Or were they placed in a hat and all the light of day excluded? If Joseph looked THROUGH the instrument, and saw the graven characters appear in succession, and the English too, it is possible that he might have known the amount of English each character made. But if he was looking at the whole page, what became of the characters that did not stand in view of the translator? Did the instrument cover the page with a mist, and only allow the propper character to appear through the mist, or does it look as though the story was fabricated out of whole cloth, and that it was not so carefully thought out that sometimes one story was told and sometimes another. In the second Martin says: "So that the translation was just as it was engraven on the plates, precisely in the language then used." This to me is a statement made at random, for as I understand translation, the thought is all that could possibly have been reproduced; and as Martin knew nothing of language, it was impossible to know more than that Joseph or some other power told him that such was the case. We expect to present, further on in this little work, a chapter on translation.

The spelling and punctuation is a matter of interest to me. The question is, did the heavenly instrument spell and punctuate the work for Joseph? From the extracts quoted one would be led to think the work was "correct in every particular," and as spelling and punctuation are both particulars, they must have been included. To be sure, the misspelling of many words could not lead one astray; but if the work came up, either on the instrument or on the plates, or in some divinely formed background, it must have come in script or print to have been understood by Joseph. If it came in either way, of course each word would have been spelled correctly. Probably the singular and plural of verbs would have given

Joseph the most trouble if they were not spelled for him.

With his education at the time he would not have been likely to get all these things right, and if they had been written incorrectly, the printer would have been likely to want to change them, and if they were to have insisted that God was responsible for every word, as he most assuredly would have been if the instrument furnished every word, of course he would have let it remain as God gave it. Neither love, money nor threats would have induced him to have made a change, even if he had used the singular for the plural verb, or vice versa.

The punctuation, however, is a matter of very great importance. Occasionally we meet with sentences which can be punctuated so they will not convey the idea the author wished to convey. We often get letters written without punctuation, and many times they are difficult to understand. But as a matter of history the Book of Mormon manuscript was not punctuated. The typo who set the first edition says: "We had a great deal of trouble with it. It was not punctuated at all. They did not know anything about punctuation, and we had to do that ourselves." It seems to me that God could have added the punctuation just as well as not, especially when he was doing, as Orson Pratt says, "What could be more marvelous and wonderful, than for the Lord to cause an unlearned youth to read or translate a book which the wisdom of the most wise and learned could not read?"—Orson Pratt's Works, page 298.

. Had this language been perfect, it would have been marvelous, and there is plenty of room for a perfect being to have improved even on the best, but if the most marvelous part is its clumsiness, and if the translator was not furnished with the punctuation, and had to leave so important a matter to a common scrub printer, (as Joseph F. Smith informs the writer that Grandon was, and that they could not get a first-class printer to do the work) to say the least, the work was not so marvelous as it could have been. God's way may not be as man's ways, but so far as the writer is concerned, he would have had more faith in the work if it had been "correct in every particular," a model of simplicity in English, and not need more than 3,000 amendments to make it passable among even scrub English scholars. My faith would have been greater if the words "Carefully revised by the translator" had not appeared in the title page of each edition except the first as far as the fourth. We close this subject with an extract set without paragraphs or punctuation:

And now Abinadi said unto them I would that ye should understand that God himself shall come down among the children of men and shall redeem his people and because he dwelleth in flesh he shall be called the Son of God and having subjected the flesh to the will of the Father being the Father and the Son the Father because he was conceived by the power of God and the Son because of the flesh thus becoming the Father and the Son and they are one God yea the very eternal Father of heaven and of earth and thus the flesh becoming subject to the spirit or the Son to the Father being one God suffereth temptation and yieldeth not to the temptation but suffereth himself to be mocked and scourged and cast out and disowned by his people and after all this after working many mighty miracles among the children of men he shall be led yea even as Isaiah said as a sheep before the shearer is dumb so he opened not his mouth yea even so shall he be led crucified and slain the flesh becoming subject even unto death the will of the Son being swallowed up in the will of the Father and thus God breaketh the bands of death having gained the victory over death giving the Son power to make intercession for the children of men having ascended into heaven having the bowels of mercy being filled with compassion towards the children of men standing betwixt them and justice having broken the bands of death taken upon himself their iniquity and their transgressions having redeemed them and satisfied the demands of justice and now I say unto you who shall declare his generation behold I say unto you that when his soul has been made an offering for sin he shall see his seed and now what say ye and who shall be his seed

We must go over these extracts for another point, the most important of all to me. Number four says: "Until the writing was CORRECT IN EVERY PARTICULAR the words last given would remain before the eyes of the translator, and not disappear. But on the necessary corrections being made, they would immediately pass away and be succeeded by others." Number two says: "And if CORRECTLY written, that sentence would disappear and another appear in its place. But if not written CORRECTLY it remained until CORRECT-

ED." Number one says: "There were no delays over obscure passages, no difficulties over the choice of words, no stoppages from the ignorance of the translator; no time was wasted in investigation or argument over the value intent or meaning of certain characters, and there were no references to authorities. These difficulties to human work were removed. All was as simple as when a clerk writes from dictation. The translation of the characters appeared on the Urim and Thummim, sentence by sentence, and as soon as one was CORRECTLY transcribed the next would appear."

This is one point of history where there is no disagreement in testimony so far as I have been able to learn. Joseph was furnished with every syllable. He did not have to ransack his scanty vocabulary for the proper word. "It was all as simple as when a clerk writes from dictation," when the dictator reads from a printed page. If he could not pronounce it he could spell it, and it did not matter whether he knew the meaning or not.

If language could be made stronger than the above in proof that Joseph had every word furnished him by the instrument, it is given in the following:

REVELATION.

(Sec. 10 Present Edition. Sec. 9 First Edition, D. & C.)

Revelation given to Joseph Smith, jun., in Harmony, Pennsylvania, May, 1829, informing him of the alteration of the Manuscript of the fore part of the Book of Mormon.

1. Now, behold, I say unto you, that because you delivered up those [so many] writings which you had power given unto you to translate, by the means of the Urim and Thummim, into the hands of a wicked man, you have lost them;

2. And you also lost your gift at the same time, and your mind became darkened.

3. Nevertheless, it is now [has been] restored unto

[NOTE—The parts set in light face type and enclosed in brackets have been eliminated since the first edition, in 1833. The parts set in light face type and not enclosed in brackets have been added since the first edition.]

you again, therefore see that you are faithful and continue [go] on unto the finishing of the remainder of the work of translation as you have begun.

4. Do not run faster, or labor more than you have strenth and means provided to enable you to translate; but be diligent unto the end:

5. Pray always, that you may come off conquereror; yea, that you may conquer Satan, and that you may escape the hands of the servants of Satan [and those] that do uphold his work.

6. Behold, they have sought to destroy you; yea, even the man in whom you have trusted, has sought to destroy you.

7. And for this cause I said that he is a wicked man, for he has sought to take away the things wherewith you have been entrusted; and he has also sought to destroy your gift;

8. And because you have delivered the writings into his hands, behold, wicked men [they] have taken them from you:

9. Therefore, you have delivered them up; yea, that which was sacred unto wickedness.

10. And, behold, Satan has put it into their hearts to alter the words which you have caused to be writen, or which you have translated, which have gone out of your hands.

11. And, behold, I say unto you, that because

they have altered the words, they read contrary from that which you translated and caused to be written;

12. And on this wise, the devil has sought to lay a cunning plan, that he may destroy this work;

13. For he has put it into their hearts to do this, that by lying they may say they have caught you in the words which you have pretended to translate.

14. Verily, I say unto you, that I will not suffer that Satan shall accomplish his evil design in this thing.

15. For, behold, he has put it into their hearts to get thee to tempt the Lord thy [their] God, in asking to translate it over again;

16. And then, behold, they say and think [for behold they say] in their hearts, we will see if God has given him power to translate, if so, he will also give him power again;

17. And if God giveth him power again, or if he translates [translate] again, or in other words, if he bringeth forth the same words, behold, we have the same with us, and we have altered them:

18. Therefore, they will not agree, and we will say that he has lied in his words, and that he has no gift, and that he has no power:

19. Therefore we will destroy him and also the work, and we will do this that we may not be

ashamed in the end, and that we may get glory of the world.

20. Verily, verily, I say unto you, that Satan has great hold upon their hearts; he stirreth them up to [do] iniquity against that which is good,

21. And their hearts are corrupt and full of wickedness and abominations, and they love darkness rather than light, because their deeds are evil: therefore they will not ask of me.

22. Satan stirreth them up, that he may lead their souls to destruction.

23. And thus he has laid a cunning plan, thinking to destroy the work of God, but I will require this at their hands, and it shall turn to their shame and condemnation in the day of judgment.

24. Yea, he stirreth up their hearts to anger against this work;

25. Yea, he saith unto them, deceive and lie in wait to catch, that ye may destroy: behold, this is no harm, and thus he flattereth them, and telleth them that it is no sin to lie, that they may catch a man in a lie, that they may destroy him.

26. And thus he flattereth them, and leadeth them along until he draggeth their souls down to hell; and thus he causeth them to catch themselves in their own snare.

27. And thus he goeth up and down, to and fro in the earth, seeking to destroy the souls of men.

28. Verily, verily, I say unto you, wo be unto him that lieth to deceive, because he supposeth that another lieth to deceive, for such are not exempt from the justice of God.

29. Now, behold, they have altered these [those] words, because Satan saith unto them, He hath deceived you: and thus he flattereth them away to do iniquity, to get thee to tempt the Lord thy [their] God.

30. Behold, I say unto you, that you shall not translate again those words which have gone forth out of your hands:

31. For behold, they shall not accomplish their evil designs in lying [lie any more] against those words. For behold, if you should bring forth the same words, they will [would] say that you have lied; that you have pretended to translate, but that you have contradicted yourself; [your words]

32. And, behold, they will [would] publish this, and Satan will [would] harden the hearts of the people to stir them up to anger against you, that they will [might] not believe my words.

33. Thus Satan thinketh to [would] overpower your testimony in this generation, that the work may [might] not come forth in this generation:

34. But behold, here is wisdom, and because I show unto you wisdom, and give you commandments concerning these things, what you shall do, show it not unto the world until you have accomplished the work of translation.

Please note the language of the tenth verse, "Satan has put it into their hearts to alter the words which you have caused to be written." Also the eleventh, "because they have altered the words that they read contrary from that which you have translated." Notice the thirteenth. The people who had the manuscript were going to lie by claiming that Joseph had not translated the work over again exactly as it was at first. Of course Joseph could translate it again word for word; but what was the use? The people would change the work, causing it to read "contrary." In my way of looking at it, language could not be put up setting forth the claim that Joseph was furnished every word, and if he was, we simply refer you to the next chapter, showing the changes he made himself after the book had been published to the world. Surely there can be no harm in wondering if this is a cunning plan laid by Satan, as set forth in verses twelve and thirteen.

Changes of the Book of Mormon.

In presenting this subject we wish to call attention to the fact that the work of comparing the books was a long, tedious job for a working man. Many hours were spent at the work when the eyes refused to stand guard as they should, desiring more to be locked in slumber. Therefore it is quite probable that all the mistakes are not noted; but we feel quite sure there are none here mentioned which do not occur.

Where figures do not follow the correction it occurs but once; where they do follow they tell the number of times they do occur. We did not use quotation marks to enclose the parts inserted or taken out, because there were not enough in the office:

I BOOK OF NEPHI.

Which to who	76
Which to whom	6
Which to that	
Saith to said	25
Saith to say	
Them to those	3
They to them	
They to those	13
Was to were	9
Is to are	3
Hath to has	3
Had to has	5
Hath to have	3
Hath to had	
That eliminated	61
Was to are	
That which eliminated	
That he eliminated	
Saith the prophet eliminated	
And eliminated	
Do eliminated	
My to thy	
Knowing to know	
Thou to ye	2
Might to may	
Our to my	
Them to those	
How to what	
Had eliminated	2
Desirous to desirable	
In my dream eliminated	
To eliminated	
And after I had followed him eliminated	
In eliminated	
Yea to and	
Only eliminated	
How eliminated	
And I beheld eliminated	
It be eliminated	
Yea eliminated	2
Remember to remberest	
Should to are	
Dominion to dominions	

They should to to	
All eliminated	
Speak that to saith	
Lieth to lies	
And it came to pass eliminated	
Telleth to tells	
For all men added	
As if to that	
Wherefore eliminated	2
To eliminated	
Sat to set	
The son of added	3
Much eliminated	
Exceeding to exceedingly	
Judgment to judgments	
They added	
Of to with	
For to and	
Remembereth to rememberest	
Wherefore eliminated	
Jesus Christ to the Messiah	
Called to call	
Founder to foundation	
And eliminated	
Them to all those	
Commandment to commandments	
Behold after this eliminated	
Before to behold	
And eliminated	
After that I eliminated	
The to their	
That shall publish to yea	
State of awful woundedness to awful state of blindness	
And if it so be that they harden not their hearts against the Lamb of God eliminated	
If it so be that to and if	
Of God eliminated	
Did lose me not to did not lose me	

I should have perished also eliminated

II BOOK OF NEPHI.

Which to who 63
That to who 8
Saith to said
Sayeth to said 3
Saith to says
They to those 30
Was to were
were to was
Is to are 3
Are to is
Hath to has 14
Hath to have 4
Hast to have
Thou to ye
Thinketh to thinks
It came to pass that
That eliminated 30
Belongeth to belongs
Cometh to comes
And eliminated
Is to their
Know to knows
Wherefore to and
Horner to homer
Constrain to restrain
From to of
My to thy
Of eliminated
Right eliminated
My father inserted
Spake to spoken
The to his
Notwithstanding eliminated
That ye shall to have him to
Do eliminated
That they should to to
Therefore eliminated
Hath me to has
Them eliminated
Wherefore eliminated
Believeth to believe
Come to came
Appointed to opened
Kindleth to kindle
Bare to bear
It to he 2
Have to I
If it it so be that eliminated

Got to gotten
Amoz to Amos 3
Not inserted
Am inserted 2
Is into inserted
Convert to be converted
And to that
Remaliah to Remalia 5
The eliminated
Aside to away.
Zion to Sion
And inserted
Lands to land
Had eliminated
Yieldeth to yield
Founder to foundation 2
Causeth to cause
Unto to to
Things to words
I cannot hope to can I hope

BOOK OF JACOB.

Which to who 5
Sayeth to said 35
Saith to said 4
They to those
Hath to has 4
Hath to have
That eliminated 5
They to them
Done to did
They to the
Ascendeth to ascend
Shall eliminated
About inserted
To it eliminated
Wherefore eliminated
Never to ever

BOOK OF ENOS.

That eliminated
And the words of my father eliminated
Sayeth to said 2
Not to never before
Passeth to pass
It eliminated
Much to many

BOOK OF JAROM.

Which to who

CHANGES OF THE

BOOK OF OMNI.
Not eliminated

WORDS OF MORMON.
That eliminated
Has to have
Wherefore they eliminated

BOOK OF MOSIAH.
Which to who	40
Which to whom	4
Saith to said	26
Was to were	30
Is to are	7
Hath to has	35
Hath to have	10
Hath to had	3
That eliminated	3
Done to did	3
Any to no	2
Doth to do	
Thou to ye	6
Beholdest to behold	
Flames to flame	
Dwelleth to dwell	
Drinketh to drink	
Believeth to believe	
Repenteth to repent	
Afflictions to affliction	
Has to have	2
Hath eliminated	
Spake to spoken	
Prophesying to prophecy	
Hast to has	
Desireth to desire	
Teachest to teach	
Knowest to know	
Had eliminated	
Sayest to say	
That to who	2
That to and	
There to these	
Had eliminated	
Rebelleth to rebel	
Dieth to die	
Hath to his	
Desires to desire	
They eliminated	
For eliminated	
The ones who to which	
Benjaman to Mosiah	

It came to pass that eliminated	10
Thee to you	
When eliminated	
For to and	
May to mayest	
Them to those	
Sayeth to says	
Repenteth to repents	
Commanding to commanded	
Much to many	
Remained to remain	
No to any	
According to the crime which he hath committed	
Cometh to comes	
Seeth to sees	
Remaineth to remains	
Had not eliminated	
Not inserted	
Their to his	

BOOK OF ALMA.
Which to who	195
Which to whom	13
Which to when	
That to who	
Who to which	
Saith to said	106
Sayeth to said	2
Sayeth to say	
Was to were	50
These to those	
Were to was	2
Nor to or	
Is to are	10
Hath to has	57
Hath to have	5
Hath to had	
That eliminated	4
Done to did	4
Doth to do	3
Doth eliminated	9
Had eliminated	
Come to came	
They to them	
The eliminated	
Him to he	
Being to were	
A eliminated	
His to their	
Seeing to he saw	

BOOK OF MORMON. 45

Now eliminated
Word to words
For eliminated 8
Not el minated
Up eliminated
Not inserted
He eliminated 2
Got to gotten
And to but
And eliminated 4
Art to is
Whomsoever to whosoever 2
Arriven to arrived
Affections to affection
Fell to fallen 2
Binds to bind
Slew to slain
Suffer to succour
To to at
To eliminated
It came to pass that eliminated 21
Causeth to caused
Know to known
He hath to has he
And Amon to he
Which was to those who were
My to thy
Judgeth to judged
And to an
Oweth to owed
Desires to desire
Receiveth to received
Kind to kinds
Answereth to answered
Smote to smitten
Durst to dare
Their to our
Had not ought to ought not
Having to have
No to any
And to now
Arrest to wrest
Becometh to becomes
Also eliminated
Delighteth to delight
Stronger to strong
Was also to also was
Thee to you
Taking to taken
Where to whence
Respects to respect

No eliminated
Even as with power and authority eliminated
Causeth to causes
If to will
Fell to fallen
War eliminated
Art to are
Humbleth to humble
Might to may
Promise to promises
Nevertheless eliminated
Its to their
To eliminated
Him to he
Of eliminated
Became to become
Cherubims to cherubim
Therefore eliminated
And Moroni eliminated
Came to come
It came to pass that Moroni and his army eliminated
Have fought to fight
Saying eliminated
Wrote to written
Devices to device
Which was subsequent to to which men were subject
Son to sons

BOOK OF HELAMAN.

Which to who 96
Which to whom 3
That to who
Saith to said
Saith to say
Them to those
Was to were 6
Were to was 3
Is to are
Is to art
Hath to has 22
Hath to have 4
Doth to do 2
They to those
Those to these
He eliminated
Neither to either
Contentions to contention
Nobler to robber
Buildeth to build

CHANGES OF THE

Fa e to faces
For eliminated
In eliminated
Whatsoever was eliminated
Repenteth to repent
Ways to way
And eliminated 5
Hideth to hide
Him to eliminated
Many-day to many days
In to into
Hideth to hide
Treasure to treasures
Arriven to arrived
Ye will eliminated
Layeth to lay
Came to come
Those to them

III BOOK OF NEPHI.

Which to who 136
Which to whom 15
Sayeth to said 23
Saith to said 2
Them to those 5
Was to were 6
Were to was 3
Is to are 7
Has to hath
Hath to have 4
That eliminated 2
They to those 6
Them to those
Them to they
Sign to signal
Which was between the land of Zarahemla and the eliminated
Were to had
Testifies to testify
Drank to drunk
Of which to whom
Spake to spoken 5
In to on
Out eliminated
And eliminated
Repenteth to repent
It came to pass eliminated
Eat to eaten 2
Their to his 3
Healings to healing
Wrote to written

Had eliminated
Traveleth to travel
Sufficiently to sufficient
Gives to give
To get gain inserted
For to get gain eliminated

IV BOOK OF NEPHI.

Which to who 11
They to those
Was to were 2
Were to was
No eliminated 3
Their el minated

BOOK OF MORMON.

Which to who 32
Which to whom
Saith to said
That to who
Was to were 3
Were to was 3
Is to are 4
They to those 2
Hath to have 2
That eliminated
A eliminated
This to these
Them to him
Rumders to murders
The eliminated
Taat to him
Which eliminated
Of to both
Of eliminated
Beaz to Boaz
I eliminated
Remaineth to remain
Their eliminated
Not eliminated
They have to he has
They do to he does
That which eliminated
The eliminated
None to no
And because that none other people knoweth our language eliminated

BOOK OF ETHER.

Which to who 47
Which to whom 3

BOOK OF MORMON. 47

Saith to said		
Was to were	2	
Were to was	5	
Is to are	3	
Hath to has		
That eliminated		
Speaketh to speaks		
Of eliminated		
Clowd to cloud		
The eliminated		
Decree to decrees		
This to these		
Not eliminated		
For eliminated		
Knew to might know		
Benjaman to Mosiah		
Wrote to written		
Them to him	2	
He eliminated		
The eliminated	12	
In the which to and	2	
Much to many		
Slew to slain		
A eliminated	2	
Avengeth to avenge		
The Lord to He		
In the to by		
In the to with		

Do eliminated	
Whereunto to but	
Did to didst	
Rememberest to remember	
How eliminated	
Dwelleth to dwell	
Garment to garments	
They eliminated	

BOOK OF MORONI.

Which to who	6
That to who	2
Was to were	2
Hath to has	2
Hath to have	
That eliminated	8
Doth to do	
Surely to sure	
They to those	
Needeth to need	2
Of eliminated	
Had not ought to ought not	
The eliminated	
Has to have	
And eliminated	
Comes to come	

We present a few sentences with the changes in, that the reader can see how the changes appear in the book:

"Which" to "Who" and "They" to "Those."

I NEPHI 22: 23. For the time speedily shall come, that all churches which are built up to get gain, and all those who [they which] are built up to get power over the flesh and those who [they which] are built up to become popular in the eyes of the world, and those who [they which] seek the lusts of the flesh and the things of the world, and to do all manner of iniquity; yea, in fine, all those who [they which] belong to the kingdom of the devil, are they who [which] need fear and quake; they are those who [they which] must be brought low in the dust; they are those who [they which] must be consumed as stubble; and this is according to the words of the prophet.

ALMA 57: 18-27. Those men whom [which] we sent. And those men who [which] had been selected. My men who [which] had been wounded. Out of my two thousand and sixty, who [which] had fainted. Not one soul of them who [which] did perish; yea, and neither was there one soul among them who [which] had not received many wounds. Our brethren who [which] were slain. Now this was the faith of those of whom [which]

III NEPHI 6: 21. Now there were many of the people who [which] were exceeding angry because of those who [which] testified of these things; and those who [which] were angry were chiefly the chief judges, and they who [which] had been high priests and lawyers, all those who [they which] were lawyers, were angry with those who [which] testified of these things.

23. Now there were many of those who [which] testified of the things pertaining to Christ, who [which] testified boldly, who [which] were taken and put to death secretly by the judges, that the knowl-

edge of their death came not unto the governor of the land, until after their death.

"Saith" to "Said."

• JACOB 7:9. And I said [sayeth] unto him, Deniest thou the Christ who should come? And he said [sayeth], If there should be a Christ, I would not deny him; but I know that there is no Christ, neither has been, nor ever [never] will be.

10. And I said [sayeth] unto him, Believest thou the scriptures? And he said [sayeth], Yea.

11. And I said [sayeth] unto him,

ALMA 45:2. And it came to pass in the nineteenth year of the reign of the judges over the people of Nephi, that Alma came to his son Helaman and said [saith] unto him, Believest thou the words which I spake unto thee concerning those records which have been kept?

3. And Helaman said [saith] unto him, Yea, I believe.

4. And Alma said [saith] again, Believest thou in Jesus Christ, who [which] shall come?

5. And he said [saith], Yea, I believe all the words which thou hast spoken.

6. And Almy said [saith] unto him again, Will ye keep my commandments?

7. And he said, Yea I will keep thy commandments with all my heart.

8. And Alma said [saith] unto him, Blessed art thou;

Double Negatives.

II NEPHI 33: 9. But behold, for none of these can I hope [I cannot hope],

OMNI I: 17. And Mosiah, nor the people of Mosiah, could]not] understand them.

MOSIAH 3: 17. That there shall be no other name given, nor any [no] other way nor means whereby *

29: 14. Nor any [no] manner of iniquity:

ALMA 29: 2. That there might not be [no] more sorrow upon all the face of the earth.

23: 7. That they did not fight against God any [no] more,

HELAMAN 1: 31. And now behold the Lamanites could not retreat either [neither] way;

Miscellaneous.

I NEPHI 8: 7. And it came to pass that as I followed him, [and after I had followed him] I beheld myself that I was in a dark and dreary waste.

11: 13. I beheld a virgin, and she was exceedingly [exceeding] fair and white.

18. And he said unto me, Behold the virgin whom

BOOK OF MORMON. 51

[which] **thou seest, is the mother of** the son of God; after the manner of the flesh.

21. And the angel said unto me, Behold the Lamb of God; Yea, even the son of the Eternal Father.

32. And I looked and beheld the Lamb of God, that he was taken by the people; yea, the son of the everlasting God was judged of the world.

13: 32. Neither will the Lord God suffer that the Gentiles shall for ever remain in that awful state of blindness [state of awful woundedness) which thou beholdest (that) they are in because of the plain and most precious parts of the gospel of the Lamb which have(hath) been kept back by that abominable church, whose foundation thou hast seen.

II NEPHI 5: 3. Our younger brother thinks (thinketh) to rule over us. * * We will not have him to (that he shall) be our ruler; for it belongs (belongeth) unto us, who (which) are the elder brethren to rule over this people.

15. And I did teach my people, to (that they should) build buildings.

17. And it came to pass that I, Nephi, did cause my people to (that they should) be industrious, and to (that they should) labor with their hands.

II NEPHI 8: ISAIAH 51: 9. Awake, awake! Put on strength, O arm of the Lord; awake as in the ancient days. Art thou not he (it) that hath cut Rahab, wounded the dragon?

10. Art thou not he who (it which) hath dried the sea.

23. But I will put it into the hand of them that afflict thee who have (which I) said to thy soul.

II NEPHI 12: ISIAH 2: 9. And the mean man boweth not down, and the great man humbleth himself not, therefore forgive him not.

MOSIAH 18: 8. Here are (is) the waters of Mormon.

10. If this be the desire (desires) of your hearts.

11. This is the desire (desires) of our hearts.

ALMA 1: 30. And thus in their prosperous circumstances, they did not send away any who were (which was) naked, or that were (was) hungry, or that were (was) athirst, or that were (was) sick.

17. And now the law could have no power on any man for his (their) belief.

2: 10. And this he did (done) that he might subject them to him.

12. Therefore the people of the Nephites were (was) aware of the intent of the Amlicites, and therefore they did prepare (for) to meet them.

10: 7. As I was (a) journeying.

8. And as I was (a) going thither.

30: 56. But he was cast out, and went about from

BOOK OF MORMON. 47

Saith to said	2
Was to were	5
Were to was	3
Is to are	
Hath to has	
That eliminated	
Speaketh to speaks	
Of eliminated	
Clowd to cloud	
The eliminated	
Decree to decrees	
This to these	
Not eliminated	
For eliminated	
Knew to might know	
Benjaman to Mosiah	
Wrote to written	
Them to him	2
He elminated	
The eliminated	12
In the which to and	2
Much to many	
Slew to slain	
A eliminated	2
Avengeth to avenge	
The Lord to He	
In the to by	
In the to with	
Do eliminated	
Whereunto to but	
Did to didst	
Rememberest to remember	
How eliminated	
Dwelleth to dwell	
Garment to garments	
They eliminated	

BOOK OF MORONI.

Which to who	6
That to who	2
Was to were	2
Hath to has	2
Hath to have	
That eliminated	8
Doth to do	
Surely to sure	
They to those	
Needeth to need	2
Of eliminated	
Had not ought to ought not	
The eliminated	
Has to have	
And eliminated	
Comes to come	

We present a few sentences with the changes in, that the reader can see how the changes appear in the book:

"Which" to "Who" and "They" to "Those."

I NEPHI 22: 23. For the time speedily shall come, that all churches which are built up to get gain, and all those who [they which] are built up to get power over the flesh and those who [they which] are built up to become popular in the eyes of the world, and those who [they which] seek the lusts of the flesh and the things of the world, and to do all manner of iniquity; yea, in fine, all those who [they which] belong to the kingdom of the devil, are they who [which] need fear and quake; they are those who [they which] must be brought low in the dust; they are those who [they which] must be consumed as stubble; and this is according to the words of the prophet.

ALMA 57: 18-27. Those men whom [which] we sent. And those men who [which] had been selected. My men who [which] had been wounded. Out of my two thousand and sixty, who [which] had fainted. Not one soul of them who [which] did perish; yea, and neither was there one soul among them who [which] had not received many wounds. Our brethren who [which] were slain. Now this was the faith of those of whom [which]

III NEPHI 6: 21. Now there were many of the people who [which] were exceeding angry because of those who [which] testified of these things; and those who [which] were angry were chiefly the chief judges, and they who [which] had been high priests and lawyers, all those who [they which] were lawyers, were angry with those who [which] testified of these things.

23. Now there were many of those who [which] testified of the things pertaining to Christ, who [which] testified boldly, who [which] were taken and put to death secretly by the judges, that the knowl-

edge of their death came not unto the governor of the land, until after their death.

"Saith" to "Said."

• JACOB 7:9. And I said [sayeth] unto him, Deniest thou the Christ who should come? And he said [sayeth], If there should be a Christ, I would not deny him; but I know that there is no Christ, neither has been, nor ever [never] will be.

10. And I said [sayeth] unto him, Believest thou the scriptures? And he said [sayeth], Yea.

11. And I said [sayeth] unto him,

ALMA 45:2. And it came to pass in the nineteenth year of the reign of the judges over the people of Nephi, that Alma came to his son Helaman and said [saith] unto him, Believest thou the words which I spake unto thee concerning those records which have been kept?

3. And Helaman said [saith] unto him, Yea, I believe.

4. And Alma said [saith] again, Believest thou in Jesus Christ, who [which] shall come?

5. And he said [saith], Yea, I believe all the words which thou hast spoken.

6. And Almy said [saith] unto him again, Will ye keep my commandments?

7. And he said, Yea I will keep thy commandments with all my heart.

8. And Alma said [saith] unto him, Blessed art thou;

Double Negatives.

II NEPHI 33: 9. But behold, for none of these can I hope [I cannot hope].

OMNI I: 17. And Mosiah, nor the people of Mosiah, could]not] understand them.

MOSIAH 3: 17. That there shall be no other name given, nor any [no] other way nor means whereby *

29: 14. Nor any [no] manner of iniquity:

ALMA 29: 2. That there might not be [no] more sorrow upon all the face of the earth.

23: 7. That they did not fight against God any [no] more,

HELAMAN 1: 31. And now behold the Lamanites could not retreat either [neither] way;

Miscellaneous.

I NEPHI 8: 7. And it came to pass that as I followed him, [and after I had followed him] I beheld myself that I was in a dark and dreary waste.

11: 13. I beheld a virgin, and she was exceedingly [exceeding] fair and white.

18. And he said unto me, Behold the virgin whom

[which] thou seest, is the mother of the son of God; after the manner of the flesh.

21. And the angel said unto me, Behold the Lamb of God; Yey, even the son of the Eternal Father.

32. And I looked and beheld the Lamb of God, that he was taken by the people; yea, the son of the everlasting God was judged of the world.

13: 32. Neither will the Lord God suffer that the Gentiles shall for ever remain in that awful state of blindness [state of awful woundedness) which thou beholdest (that) they are in because of the plain and most precious parts of the gospel of the Lamb which have(hath)been kept back by that abominable church, whose foundation thou hast seen.

II NEPHI 5: 3. Our younger brother thinks (thinketh) to rule over us. * * We will not have him to (that he shall) be our ruler; for it belongs (belongeth) unto us, who (which) are the elder brethren to rule over this people.

15. And I did teach my people, to (that they should) build buildings.

17. And it came to pass that I, Nephi, did cause my people to (that they should) be industrious, and to (that they should) labor with their hands.

II NEPHI 8: ISAIAH 51: 9. Awake, awake! Put on strength, O arm of the Lord; awake as in the ancient days. Art thou not he (it) that hath cut Rahab, wounded the dragon?

10. Art thou not he who (it which) hath dried the sea.

23. But I will put it into the hand of them that afflict thee who have (which I) said to thy soul.

II NEPHI 12: ISIAH 2: 9. And the mean man boweth not down, and the great man humbleth himself not, therefore forgive him not.

MOSIAH 18: 8. Here are (is) the waters of Mormon.

10. If this be the desire (desires) of your hearts.

11. This is the desire (desires) of our hearts.

ALMA 1: 30. And thus in their prosperous circumstances, they did not send away any who were (which was) naked, or that were (was) hungry, or that were (was) athirst, or that were (was) sick.

17. And now the law could have no power on any man for his (their) belief.

2: 10. And this he did (done) that he might subject them to him.

12. Therefore the people of the Nephites were (was) aware of the intent of the Amlicites, and therefore they did prepare (for) to meet them.

10: 7. As I was (a) journeying.

8. And as I was (a) going thither.

30: 56. But he was cast out, and went about from

house to house (a) begging for his food.

58. And Korihor did go about from house to house (a) begging for his support.

Please note—there are 2038 places changed. That they are correcting the commonest kinds of grammatical errors. The number of both nouns and verbs is changed. Adjectives are changed for adverbs. The tense of verbs is changed. Superfluous words and clauses are eliminated. Words and clauses are added to complete or amend the sentence. Pronouns are changed. The ancient form is changed to the modern in hundreds of places, sometimes as many as thirteen times on a single page. Sometimes the word "saith" is spelled "sayeth".

A passing notice of the pages of changes is not sufficient if we wish to

[NOTE—The parts set in light face type and enclosed in brackets have been eliminated since the first edition, in 1833. The parts set in light face type and not enclosed in brackets have been added since the first edition.]

understand how the book has been revised. In fact one cannot realize the extent of the changes unless he can see a book with the changes marked. While in some of the illustrative sentences quoted the mistakes are somewhat thicker than the average, it will be noticed that there must be an average of almost four to the page. The changes are less frequent in the parts claimed to have been taken from the plates brought from Jerusalem when King James has it in his translation too. This makes the average of original parts greater. The phrase, "It came to pass" has been stricken out in a number of places.

What a Translation is.

Some people may think I am presumptuous to write under such a heading as the above, because I have not had a college education, and understand no tongue but the English, and that very impefectly. But let it be here suggested that we often have things to investigate that we are not professors of. In fact there are so few people who master more than one branch of science that were it not for this fact we would not be allowed to speak upon the general subjects of the day. But as a matter of fact we are surrounded by things and subjects that we must, in part at least, make up our minds on—we must pass an opinion.

As a rule there is a way for any of us to investigate any subject we need, and obtain a fair understanding of it. We will get at it in our way. So in investigating the subject before us, it is not necessary for one to go through the various languages and understand all the "ins" and "outs" of translation.

Usually there is some special object to be attained in presenting a subject, and often that object can be attained by investigating only a small part of the great field that would occupy the mind of a careful student or scientist. So with the work at hand. The object being to see if the grammatical errors which may have been made by the Nephites could, would or should have been reproduced in the English translation of our times.

The ancient writers confess their ignorance of writing and apoligize to this generation. If the book is what it purports to be, we should excuse and most heartily thank them for having done the best they could for our information. We give their apology.

I NEPHI 1: 1. I, Nephi, having been born of goodly parents, therefore I was taught somewhat in all the learning of my father; and having seen many afflictions in the course of my days —nevertheless, having been highly favored of the Lord in all my days; yea, having had a great knowledge of the goodness and the mysteries of God, therefore I make a record of my proceedings in my days;

2. Yea, I make a record in the language of my father, which consists of the learning of the Jews, and the language of the Egyptians.

3. And I know that the record which I make is true; and I make it with mine own hand; and I make it according to my knowledge.

MORMON 9: 31. Condemn me not because of mine imperfection; neither my father, because of his imperfection; neither them who (which) have written before him, but rather give thanks unto God that he hath made manifest unto you our imperfections, that ye may learn to be more wise than (that which) we have been.

32. And now behold, we have written this record according to our knowledge in the characters, which are called among us the reformed Egyptian, being handed down and altered by us according to our manner of speech.

33. And if our plates had been sufficiently large, we should have written in (the) Hebrew; but the Hebrew hath been altered by us also; and if we could have written in (the) Hebrew, behold, ye would have had no (none) imperfection in our record.

34. But the Lord knoweth the things which we have written, and also that none other people knoweth our language, (and because that none other people knoweth our language,) therefore he hath prepared means for the interpretation thereof.

35. And these things are written, that we may rid our garments of the blood of our brethren who (which) have dwindled in unbelief.

MORMON 8: 12. And whoso receiveth this record and shall not condemn it because of the imperfections which are in it, the same shall know of greater things than these. Behold, I am Moroni; and were it possible, I would make all things known unto you,

17. And if there be faults, they be the faults of a man. But behold, we know no fault. Nevertheless God knoweth all things; therefore he that condemneth, let him be aware lest he shall be in danger of hell fire.

Seven sentences have been selected from the first edition of the Book of Mormon, containing a variety of mistakes which have been corrected. Copies of these sentences were sent to Professors of languages with the simple request to translate. One was asked to translate into German, another into French, and the other into Latin. The last two were kindly furnished, but the German did not come. We illustrate our point with the two.

Other Professors were now asked to translate the Latin and French back into English. So we here submit the three Englishes, the Latin and the French.

From the First Edition.

1. "The servant done according to his word."
2. "The Lord of the vineyard saith again unto his servant."

3. "He had been a preparing the minds of the people."

4. "He was acknowledged king throughout all the land, among all the people of the Lamanites, which was composed of the Lamanites."

5. "I have wrote unto you."

6. "I trust that the souls of them which has been slain, have entered into the rest of their God."

7. "They retreated into the wilderness again, yea, even back the same way which they had come."

From the Latin.

1. "The servant did it from his own faith."

2. The master of the vineyard speaks again to his servant."

3. "He had prepared the minds of the people."

4. "He is called a king unto all the land among the whole people of the Lamanites who stand among the Lamanites."

5. "I wrote to you."

6. "I hope the souls of those who were killed have entered into the peace of their God."

7. They again betook themselves into the desert places; thus, even back in the very way by which they had come."

From the French.

1. "The servant acted according to his word."

2. "The master of the vineyard said again to his servant."

3. "He had prepared the minds of the people."

4. "He was recognized as king throughout all the country among all the people of the Lamanites."

5. "I have written to you."

6. "I believe that the souls of those who have been killed have entered into the repose of their God."

7. "They withdrew again into the desert; yea, by the same route over which they had come."

French.

1. Le serviteur agit selon sa parole.
2. Le maitre de la vigne dit encore a son serviteur.
3. Il avait prepare les esprits du peuple.
4. Il etait reconnu comme roi tout au travers du pays, parmi tout le peuple des Lamanites.
5. Je vous ai ecrit.
6. Je crois que les ames de ceux qui ont ete tues, sont entres dans le repos de leur Dieu.
7 Ils se sont retires encore dans le desert, oui, par la meme route sur laquelle ils etaient venus.

Latin.

1. Servus ex fide suo fecit.
2. Dominus vineae servo suo iterum dicit.
3. Animos populorum praeparaverat.
4. Ille rex appellatur in terram totam inter omnem populum Laminitum qui in Laminitibus constitit.

5. Ad te scripsi.

6. Spero animos illorum qui necati sunt in pacem Dei suorum inisse.

7. In loca deserta iterum se receperunt; ita, etiam retro in via ipsa qua venerant.

At this point it is quite probable that some readers would enjoy a criticism of the grammatical construction of the original sentences, and since it was furnished by the professors who translated, we feel equal to the occasion.

One of them very modestly said, "If you will allow me first to correct the English of some of the sentences that you sent I will endeavor to translate them into French."

But the other goes further and tells where each sentence is wanting.

The English Criticised.

"My second comment must be a severe criticism on the grammar of the sentences submitted. The errors are of so gross a nature as to show great ignorance on the part of the original user of the expressions or of one who habitually employs them.

The error in the first consists in the use of a perfect participle for the past-tense form. At no time in the history of the English language was such a usage permitted. So far as I am acquainted with other languages this is not now and never was permitted in them; and if a translation of the English as submitted be insisted upon, all I can say is that it can not be translated.

The second is correct.

The third while not positively incorrect is at least inelegant in the use of 'a preparing', 'a' being a preposition and 'preparing', a gerund, its object. Before translating, the "a" must be stricken out.

The error in the forth is in the use of the singular verb 'was' with a plural subject 'which', referring to 'all people'. The sentence is otherwise clumsy. In no language does a plural word as a subject take a singular predicate.

The error in the fifth is in the use of a past-tense form 'wrote' for a perfect participle 'written'. This is nowhere permitted.

The sixth also contains a plural subject, 'which' with a singular predicate, 'has been slain'.

The seventh is clumsy in the omission of needed prepositions before 'same way' and before 'which' respectively."

Some people who are acquainted with language and can see at a glance where the English of the first edition is faulty, may think we are pursuing these little matters just to fill up space. But the experience had up to date is of such a nature as to demand the chasing of every little point of evidence until it vanishes in the distance. Neighbors, and those too, who hold the respect of all on political and financial matters, say our language is continually undergoing a change and probably it was translated correctly into the language as it was then, but has simply been changed since to keep pace with a progressive language. But hear what our Professor says of the first sentence "At no time in the history of the English language was such a usage permitted. So far as I am acquainted with other languages this is not now and never was permitted in them." Also in criticising the fourth he says. "In no language does a plural word as a subject take a singular predicate." And in the fifth. "This is nowhere permitted."

If our informant knows what he is talking about, any little consolation that our neighbors might borrow from the thought that the book was translated into correct English at first will have to vanish as the manna of the Israelites did after sunrise on all week-days.

Another point in connection with the

criticism of the first sentence is worth our consideration.

"If a translation of the English as submitted be insisted upon, all I can say is that it cannot be translated." And our other linguist said, If I would allow him to first correct the English he would translate.

If it were ever so great a crime to wonder, my mind is so framed that I can not avoid wondering what the apology of the ancient writers of the B. of M. amounts to. It is calculated to account for the bad grammar. But our modern students of language cannot translate such grammatical errors from one language to another. If we will now turn back and compare the Englishes, we will see that while they differ a little from each other the grammatical errors have been eliminated. Even those needed prepositions in the seventh have been supplied. From the French we get "by" and "over". From the Latin we get "in" and "by".

Referring to the matter of translating grammatical errors, one of the Professors informs me that there are some kinds of errors, that can be translated from one language into another, but further said that if his students were translating a sentence with a grammatical error in it he would expect them first to correct the error, unless it was a slang phrase which depended upon the error for its significance.

Besides criticising the sentences our Professor tells us briefly but plainly what a translation is.

"My first statement must be an explanation of a translation. It is not an exact setting over, word for word, from one language to another; but the using of such expressions in one language as conveys the same idea to one who speaks that language as the words of another language conveys to one who speaks that other language. Thus 'How do you do' conveys the same idea to an American as 'Wie geht's' conveys to a German; but the word for word equivalent in English of the German form is, 'How goes it'. Any Latin equivalent for English expressions must be of the same nature."

We wish here to call attention to the fact that a translation is not a "word for word" setting over from one language to another, but it is simply conveying the thoughts of one language in words conveying the same thoughts in the other. If we will compare our French, Latin and English we will observe that the words look nothing alike, we may be sure that they would sound nothing alike if spoken. And all of us have seen enough foreigners who mix up the grammatical parts of the sentence in such a way that we may know that the parts of speech are differently arranged. In fact the construction of the whole language is different. This being true what excuse is there for the thousands of grammatical errors in the first edition of the book which God himself condescends to translate that we might have his law in its purity? Why should He inspire his servants to write the following article of faith? "We believe the Bible to be the word of God, as far as it is translated correctly; we also believe the Book of Mormon to be the word of God".?

Please note in this article not one word of allowance is made for wrong translation of the B. of M.

Is such a work a marvel and a wonder in any other sense than that men would prepare it and that so many would believe it came from God. This WE are willing to admit is marvelous; and when superficially examined I felt like exclaiming in the language of King Agrippa, "Almost thou persuadest me to believe".

We might now, with profit, return to page 20 and again consider Martin Harris' statement, that the plates were translated in precisely the same language that was used by the ancients. It will be remembered that we thought he could not have understood what he was saying. That he did not know the meaning of his own words. The idea we have is, for this to be true, the "Reformed Egyptian," which was cut loose from civilization twenty-four hundred years ago, must have developed into a grammatical construction very similar to that of the English language of to-day. They may have had word signs which differed from ours in appearance, and when these words were sounded they may not have been recognizable to an ear used to the English words only. But the arrangement of the parts of speech must have been similar. This is not all, indeed it is not the half. They must have had become accustomed to making the same kinds of grammatical errors that were common in Joseph's time. Furthermore, they must have used the relative pronoun "which" for "who" just as the translators of the Bible did two hundred forty years before, which was good English at that time, but was not allowable in the days of Joseph Smith. They must have been in the habit of using a superfluous "a" as illustrated in our last four illustrative sentences, pages 52-3. Double negatives, which are directly contrary in letter to the spirit of the sentence, a common error among us, must have been common then also. In fact the errors resemble back-woods English so closely that one would be justified in rejecting the whole work on that one point alone, until conclusive evidence to the contrary is produced.

We do not wish to say positively that it is impossible for a language to have been, at that time, similar to the English of to-day. Yes it might have included the local peculiarities of Joseph's neighborhood. God is pictured to us as possessing all power. So of course he could by special design cause the ancient inhabitants of America to acquire a language of any kind He saw fit. But we do wish to express an opinion that nothing short of special interposition of the hand of Providence would have produced a language, which, when translated "precisely in the language then used," "correct in every particular," would resemble the English of Joseph's day; and even include such little grammatical errors as an illiterate person of Joseph's day would be sure to use if he wrote his own thoughts in his own way. If the work be true we have a circumstance, the like of which has never before been discovered in all the research of modern scientists.

We give below what we think the first edition should have been, coming from the source it is claimed to have come from. In this consideration we allow that the ancient writers of the book may have been ever so illiterate; and their work may have been ever so full of errors. The urim and thummim should have brought up the thoughts of the ancients. And even if these thoughts were originally clothed in language full of ambiguity it should have appeared on the urim and thummim in perfect English. We must ever bear in mind that a translation is not a setting over of words. It deals with thoughts. And be it remembered that God was producing a marvelous work and a wonder. The wisdom of the wise was to be hid because He was going to so far surpass it. The Book of Mormon, then shou'd have been a model of perfection. It should have stood out alone, a solitary pinnacle which linguists would have peeped at through a telescope from afar. It should have been a book which educators would have taken into the school room from one end of civilization to the other. No this is not asking too much. Shakspeare has stood out an unapproachable pinnacle in his line for centuries. And while he seems mighty to the scholars of today, he should have been a mere speck when compared with the work of Almighty God. The language of the Book of Mormon should have been absolutely perfect. In every case the very best word for the place should have been used. Linguists tell us that there are no synonyms, but that there is a fine shade of difference of meaning in all English words. This book, then would have been a mine of treasures. All the fine shades of meaning would have been displayed by God Himself, and all educated people would have praised the book forever more. Because any other meaning except the proper one would be impossible. Not a word could have been eliminated, added nor exchanged for another without inflicting an injury on the book. There would have been no call for such a remark as Elder Roberts made in the Bountiful meeting house in the presence of President Joseph F. Smith, at the quarterly conference, in March, 1897; that he wished the book had been changed (amended) more More than two-thousand amendments had already been made, which improved the book very much, and still God's translation is in such a shape that Elder Roberts wishes they had amended it more.

It may be urged by some that had this been the case it would be claimed that an educated person did it, and the book would be disbelieved on that account. But to this we would reply, that the claim is made that the "ALL WISE did do it. No danger of men saying that man did it. For it would have so far surpassed any thing man had done or could do that they would be obliged to look higher than man for the source. Now men say it was so full of the commonest kind of errors that an ignorant person must have done it. "There is plenty of room at the top," so if God translated the Book of Mormon it should have been on top so far clearness is concerned.

Reasons Given for Making the Changes.

After having read the testimony and seeing how very particular God was in furnishing an automatic instrument which furnished the very words to be used, and then noting how they have been changed; it seems to me that one would be justified in condemning the whole work as the scheme of an evil designing man, without asking for reasons. Under any circumstances I do not see how we can avoid asking: Why so many changes in the book after it was published to the world? Again, after one has read the Book of Mormon even casually, and noted how very particular God was to keep the plates in the hands of just men; men who could and would keep the record correct, it seems to me that he would be justified in the exclamation: Why was God so slothful at the last with his history and law? Why did He get over His bachelor notions of precision so soon? Why did He allow His book to be overhaled, amended, patched, cut, doctored, in more than two-thousand places, and still hold His peace? Why did He not come out in his wrath as He did with Uzziah for putting forth his hand to steady the ark? Or the 50,070 men of Bethshemish for simply looking into the ark? Oh! why this great change in Him who is "the same yesterday, to-day and forever?"

But one thing we should all learn if we have not learned it already; and that is always to let the accused speak for himself. For if it does no good it can do no harm. So in this case, we will let the advocates of the book speak for themselves. It may be that we have overlooked something that would clear up all this seeming contradiction of statements and circumstances. It may be that we have put altogether too much stress on the way the book was translated. We cannot tell what may come until we let the accused speak.

When we stop to gather up our scattered thoughts, and assemble the wanderings of our minds, we may remember that we don't remember of having seen a single reference to the matter in any of the church publications. We may think there are but few of our writers who know that the book has been so shamefully handled; or we may think they do not want the public to know all about such a matter, because it is not one of the "Faith Promoting Series." If any are conversant with the matter they have kept up an awful stillness; prolonged with care, the period of ignorance of the matter. But a few words have been dropped, and we will consider them though they be but few.

The preface to the second edition of the Book of Mormon is the only printed explanation why the changes were made, I have been able to find. But while investigating it, it did not satisfy me, so I wrote to Prest. Jos. F. Smith for further information. Only a small portion of the correspondence bears on the subject at hand—Reasons given for making the changes—but fearing some may think we have not quoted fairly we give all the letters. From them the reader can see the questions asked and the answers given. Then we present the preface to the second edition in full, which is all the material I have been able to find.

A Series of Letters.

BOUNTIFUL, UTAH, Jan. 17, 1897.

Joseph F. Smith, Salt Lake City, Utah.

DEAR BROTHER:—For some time past I have been growing skeptical to revealed religion. For a long time the Bible has had but one prop, that of new revelation, and now, even that, to my mind, is being weakened day by day.

The reprint of the "Doctrine and Covenants" I left with you some eighteen months ago has weakened my faith slightly. But this winter I learned that the "Book of Mormon" has been amended since the first edition. While the changes are only grammatical for the most part, when we consider how the book was translated, to my mind even grammatical changes are unpardonable.

The ward authorities know how I feel, and they think I should get down on one side of the fence or the other, which I cannot say is wrong. If I were out I should not ask to come in while I feel as I do, but since I am in I do not wish to withdraw my name until I have examined every point of evidence in my reach.

If I should learn that the Tribune had not copied

the "Doctrine and Covenants" Correctly it would strengthen my faith a little. Then if you could give a satisfactory explanation for the many grammatical changes of the "Book of Mormon" it would do much toward satisfying my mind. This done, the other little clashing points could probably be borne up by the many favorable evidences already in my possession; and I would be ready to make a full hand again in church matters.

Wednesdays or Fridays after 12, noon, would be my best time to leave school and meet with a committee you might appoint, but I will come any time you suggest, or a written reply would do as well.

Unless some change takes place it will be necessary for me to give the ward authorities an answer soon, probably in three weeks from to-day.

Hoping to hear from you soon with such a shower of evidence that my mind will be set permanently at rest. I remain desirous of being considered a Brother in the Gospel of Christ.

LAMONI CALL.

SALT LAKE CITY, UTAH, Jan. 23, 1897.
Lamoni Call. Bountiful, Davis, Co.

MY DEAR BROTHER CALL:—Your esteemed favor of the 17th inst, came to hand on the 20th and I have been so driven with duties and extraordinary pressure upon my time on account of severe sickness in my family that I have found it impossible to suitably reply to your letter. I have but a monent at my disposal now, hence this hastely written acknowledgment and my desire to express the wish that you will suspend feeling and action until I can get a few moments to write you or speak with you. Come and see me and let me speak with you regarding your views. I have a great regard for your name and ancestry and I would love to see you prosperous and happy and full of faith, knowledge and power for good. I would see you at any time I could get a moment, or I will write you later on, until then believe me your brother and friend.

Jos. F. Smith.

Bountiful, Utah, June. 27, 1897.

Joseph F. Smith, Salt Lake City, Utah.

Dear Brother: Again I am persuaded that I should write you. Since receiving yous of Jan. 23. 1897. I have called at your office several times but always found you buisy.

The ward authorities waited on me until my school quit since which time I have spent much of my time reading the Book of Mormon, and comparing the present with the first edition.

All I wish to say is that the more I read the Book the unresonable it seems to me to be. I wish it were as I onece thought it to be. It is not pleasant to cut myself off from the society of my friends, but I see no other show.

The president of the Seventies quorum said the Bishop had asked him to push things to an issue, and if I would not resign to handle me.

Now I do not wish to be handled; I have no plea to make. In my present situation I cannot think that God has done the work our people credit him with doing.

In your letter to me you asked me not to act until you saw me or wrote me, so I have delayed until now. But if I do not learn something favorable between now and next Sunday I expect to resign my position.

I enclose stap, please send my reprint of the "Covenants and Commandments".

I will come to visit you if you advise it. With kind reguards.

LAMONI CALL.

NOTE—The above letter is set just as it was written. Reference is made to the mistakes in it by Jos. F. in the following:

MAKING THE CHANGES. 87

SALT LAKE CITY, UTAH, Jun. 28, 1897.

Lamoni Call, Esq., Bountiful.

DEAR BROTHER: Your favor of the 27th inst. is duly received. I do not need to read between the lines to discover the temper of your feeling nor the condition of your mind.

I am fully persuaded that under existing conditions, with reference to your frame of mind and darkened spirit, it would be a waste of time and words for me to attempt by means of conversation or by letter to dissuade you from your intended purpose as expressed in your letter to me, or to change the trend of your thoughts by any argument, statement of facts or testimony within my power at this time. I feel quite sure that only time, experience, and the exercise of a few grains of common sense will suffice to bring about the change of heart you so much need.

I regret, probably as much as you do, the existance in the Book of Mormon as well as other church works of typographical and grammatical errors, but these are due to the imperfections of men whose handiwork in comparison to the handiwork of God is always faulty and imperfect. But this is only the evidence of man's weakness and does not destroy the perfection of God's works, nor should they impair our confidence in them. I am thankful beyond measure to know that the Gospel truths revealed through the medium of the Book of Mormon and other books accepted as authentic by the church, are divine truths and can be relied upon by every man as spiritual and intellectual guides, which if well followed will most assuredly lead him back into His presence and glory and eternal life. No amount of verbal changing or paragraphing or versing can ever shake my faith in the divine mission of Christ nor of Joseph Smith or the divine origin of the Book of Mormon, and the revelations contained in the Book of Doctrine and Covenants, or which may still remain as unpublished records in the manuscript history of the church. Especially is this so when such changes tend only to make the thought more plain, the truth more clear, and does not change or destroy its true sense. Howbeit, "the things of God knoweth no man but (by) the Spirit of God." Herein lies your mistake and consequent trouble. The scriptures are plain upon this subject. Therein it is said, "But the natural man receiveth not the things of the Spirit of God, for they are (or seem to be) foolishness unto him; neither can he know them, because they are

MAKING THE CHANGES. 89

spiritually discerned". (See 1st Cor., 2 ch., 9th to 16th ver.)

If you will humble yourself before the Lord and get a little of His Spirit in your heart, then bend your thought and effort to finding out and demonstrating the truth of the Book of Mormon and the revelations from God to Joseph Smith, instead of trying to discover whatever of error can be found in them which error, if it does exist, is only incident to the weaknesses of men, I will warrant that you will begin to see things in their true light. If you would take this course from now on, you mi_g_ht, I frimly believe, save yourself from a aserious blunder, which if you make it I can only hope that you may live long enough to discover it and repent.

With sorrow for your unfortunate mental and social condtion, and yet with sympathy and love for you as a dessendant of true, noble, and clear-sighted man, I am, with sincere regards, Your Brother,   Jos. F. Smith.

P. S. By the way I find _five_ glaring mistakes in your letter and you are "a publisher." Your letter would not make more than one fourth of a page of the B. of M. How thankful I am Joseph did not have _you_ to proof read the B. of M.! O. Cowdery was not a "publisher"!   J. F. S.

Preface to Second Edition of the Book of Mormon, Printd at Kirtland, Ohio, 1837.

"The publishers of the following volumes having obtained leave to issue five thousand copies of the same, from those holding the copyrights, would respectfully notice a few items for the benefit of the reader."

"The 1830 edition of the book of Mormon having some time since been distributed, the pressing calls for the same, as well as the book of Doctrine and Covenants, and the vast importance attached to their contents, have induced the undersigned to seek the privilege of supplying those calls by presenting in one volume, both books, in a condensed form, rendering greater convenience to elders, and others, who convey the same to different parts.

"Individuals acquainted with book printing are aware of the numerous typographical errors which always occur in manuscript editions. It is only necessary to say, that the whole has been carefully re-examined and compared with the original manuscripts, by elder Joseph Smith, Jr., the translator of the book of Mormon, assisted by the present printer, brother O. Cowdery, who formerly wrote the greatest portion of the same, as dictated by brother Smith.

MAKING THE CHANGES. 91

"Expecting, as we have reason to, that this book will be conveyed to places which circumstances will render it impossible for us to visit, and be perused by thousands whose faces we may never see on this side of eternity, we cannot consistently let the opportunity pass, without expressing our sincere conviction of its truth, and the great and glorious purposes it must effect, in the restoration of the house of Israel, and the ushering in of that blessed day when the knowledge of God will cover the earth, and one universal peace pervade all people.

PARLEY P. PRATT,
JOHN GOODSON.

"Note from back—Contrary to our expectations, when the foregoing work was commenced, we have been induced to abandon the idea of attaching to it the Book of Doctrine and Covenants. We came to this conclusion from the fact, that the two connected, would make a volume, entirely too unwieldy for the purpose intended, that of a pocket companion.

THE PUBLISHERS."

Our witnesses are few and their statments are not voluminous. So we should by a careful reading and a little thought sift it to the bottom and get the truth. At that word "truth" I realize that many of those who hold Joseph as a prophet will feel just a little indignant. The very thought of questioning his word! But let it be remembered that we are investigating, that Joseph has made a record, that that record will be investigated for a long time to come. Let those who love Joseph rest easy for the "truth will out." Many men who were considered heretics in their day are now being boosted as high as we poor mortals can boost them. All we can get is their name and record, but that is a thing that cannot be sentenced to death by a bigoted judge or a fanatical priest; or enthroned in glory by a loving mother or an earnest convert

If Joseph Smith's work was a successful fraud, the people who hold themselves open to conviction will learn the facts, but those who say, "'tis because 'tis," and, being so afraid of having their faith weaken that they positively refuse to read anything that is liable to overturn it, will remain in ignorance, and glory in that ignorance, and think it is the "power of God unto salvation." "Ignorance is bless."

If his work is just what he claims it to be, the truth is somewhere buried —from my mind at least—in the multiplied statements which seem to me to be clashing. (To say they do not clash without investigating is either lazy or cowardly. To say they do clash without investigating is just as bad.) And a careful study will bring it to the top all right. The evidence will be classified and weighed, and he will finally get full value for all the good he has done. Men will study both sides of the question and he will be given his portion among the world's greatest heroes.

So let us go to and carefully examine every point within our reach. Let us not be afraid of the scripture which says if we do not believe we will be damned, because that doctrine would make cowards of the best of us. Let me asure you that that scripture is not a heavenly truth; a Godly justice, and if it were God never would have trusted it out of heaven for fear he would be overrun with cowards.

The first edition of the book had been in circulation seven years when the second was printed. It had undoubtedly been criticised by the educated during that time. And publishers found it necessary to make a great many grammatical changes in it. The question undoubtedly arose about what they would tell the people as a reason for making the alterations in God's word. may seem to some that I am prejudging

MAKING THE CHANGES. 95

that the work is a fraud, by saying that they undoubtedly debated the matter to decide what to tell the people. The reader may think a person does not need to debate when he is going to tell simply what he knows to be the truth. But let it be remembered, the Book of Mormon was no common volume. It was the word of God; the Law of God. Surely it is not claiming too much when we assert that the publishers should have been very particular with it. And if they sent the law of God out with thousands of blunders in it the people would have the right to censure them for laziness at least. So they laid it at the door of the poor printer. They say the errors are typographical.

It seems to me that they could have added another source quite as reasonable as the above. For in the early part of the work Joseph let Martin

Harris take 116 pages of MS. home to show it to the folks, and it was lost. To avoid a repetition of so serious a matter Oliver copied the work and took it to the printer a little at a time. So the printer did not get the original copy.

It is quite reasonable to expect that Oliver would make mistakes in copying so large a work, for we have no account of his having either the seer stone or the urim and thummim to gard against errors as it did in the first copy. But the preface to the second edition makes no claim to the right to change on account of clerical errors. However, P. P. Pratt and John Goodson may not have known just what "typographical errors" included. It is possible that they thought it meant any error that Oliver or the compositor made. But one would hardly think so, for they say, "Individuals acquainted with book printing are aware of the numerous typographical errors which always occur in manuscript editions." The only reason why more typographical errors should occur in manuscript editions is on account of the liability of the printer to mistake the writer's characters.

Prest. Joseph F. says, "I regret, probably as much as you do, the existence in the Book of Mormon as well as other church works of typographical and grammatical errors. But these are due to the imperfections of men whose handiwork in comparison to the handiwork of God is always faulty and imperfect. But this is only the evidence of man's weakness and does not destroy the perfection of God's works."

Does this answer my question? I had read something much clearer than that in the preface to the second edition of the Book of Mormon. They say there that they are typographical errors, and they point out the particular book which has them. But Joseph F. simply makes a sweeping statement of all the church books. But I should like to inform him, for he seems not to know, that the Book of Mormon differs from all other books in the church if the claims for it be true. He says these errors are due to man's imperfections. Probably it would not be amiss to say that I had before read in Mormon's preface in the first edition, "and now if there are faults, it be the mistakes of men." But in the second edition he says, "they are", instead of, "it be."

In Mormon 8: 17. it says, "and if there be faults, they be the faults of a man." Which "man"? Yes indeed, well may we inquire "which man".

MAKING THE CHANGES.

Joseph F. now makes a sweeping classification of the church books in which he has the great amount of ONE group. And he regrets that they are not free from errors I should like to ask if the errors of all are traceable to the same source— man's ignorance. If so where is the handiwork of God. The handiwork of man is plainly apparent on every page. But where, in the name of that Great God that created heaven and earth is "the perfection of God's works?" That is what I have been hunting for these years. That is what I have failed to get the first glimpse of. No I have never been able to even find one of its tracks. And if I possessed the olfactory nerves of the most sensitive hound I do not belive I could even then obtain the scent of the "perfection of God's works" in all the ramifications of Mormonism.

Where God started out to produce a marvelous work and a wonder by eclipsing the wisdom of the wise we have the mistakes of "A man" and they bare all the earmarks of a very illiterate man too. With the second edition we have a progressive student, P. P. Pratt on the staff, and the revised edition is quite a credit to a man of his chances. Now we have the college graduate and the books show all the shades of difference of the men's abilities. But nowhere can "the perfection of God's works" be found.

Joseph F. can read between the lines of my letter and he sees that he will have to produce facts and since he does not think he can produce evidence which will convince me, he does not wish to waste his words on a person so likely to question everything, and believe nothing until it is proved. But I should like to call his attention to the fact that if the things of God are, or even seem to me to be, foolishness, how am I to judge them? I must judge all things as they seem to ME to be. It is impossible for ME to judge them as they seem to HIM to be. I can quote his thoughts if he makes them public, but that is all. If I get his thoughts so I can use them as my own it must be by his proving to me by facts and figures that he is right. By putting me in possession of the facts which cause him to believe or know, and then they would be my facts. I would understand them as well as he understands them. If a fact exists which cannot be proved, of what use is it? If it can only be proved to those who do not look for anything to oppose it with, of what good is it? Joseph F. suggests that I should cease to look for the opposite. What professor of mathematics would ask his students not to look for anything opposed to the rules he gives them? And until a religion can be proved with mathematical exactness we should never close our eyes to the opposite, we should never cease to ask ourselves: "Is it not possible that I might be wrong?" Thousands of people, in past ages, have proved by laying down their lives for their religion, that their faith in their religion was stronger than their love of the pleasures of this life; however feeble their evidences in support of what they believed. But we are taught by the Latter-day Saints that no people from about one hundred years after Christ's death enjoyed the saving principles of the gospel. Shall I do as they did—refuse to consider the claims of others? No! I will not. I will be free. I will investigate everything. And if God gets "mad" about it, I cannot help that. He had no business to give me a mind if He did not want me to use it.

Just a word on Joseph F's postscript. He finds five glaring mistakes in my letter. He might have found more. He is thankful that Joseph did not have me to proof read the Book of Mormon. He also informs me that Oliver Cowdry was not a publisher, and consequently he could not be expected to do a good job of proof reading.

Here he confirms the preface to the second edition, in that the mistakes are typographical, in the strongest of terms. His inference is that the manuscript, as it came from the urim and thummim was absolutely perfect. Indeed, no other claim could be made.

This being true, the only thing we need to consider is, did the printer make the errors in the first edition that have been corrected since. In other words, is our present Book of Mormon like the original manuscript as it came from the urim and thummim? If it is, the work may be true. But if it is not, the work is a fraud, as the claims of the originators of the book is not true.

Now I shall offer my reasons for believing that the errors are not typographical at all. That the present Book of Mormon is not like the first manuscript. That the errors in the first edition are traceable to the ignorance of some modern author, just as the orthographical errors of my letter are traceable to mine.

In this investigation we will be liberal. We will allow any clerical error which Oliver may have made in copying as typographical. We will allow them to bring the book to the first manuscript. But here we must insist upon a stand. No, you cannot add to, or take from that! No, not even if it does "make the thought more plain, the truth more clear." Who is to be the judge of when the thought is more plain, or the truth is more clear? Will Joseph F. set up the puny judgment of any man against that of Almighty God's? Remember, it is the duty of a translator to reproduce the thought of the language from which he is translating, in words of the language into which he is translating, which express the same thought. Then who would attempt to make a selection which he would be willing to pit against those chosen by God Himself. No sir! Most emphatically, no sir! You cannot change a single letter, even if you do think it "tends only to make the thought more plain, the truth more clear." The first manuscript or nothing for me!

In this investigation we will have to do without the first MS., because it is thought not to be in existence. David Whitmer had what he supposed was the first, but as it had the printer's marks on it, it is quite evident, in the minds of some, that it is the transcription. What is supposed to be the original copy, with other papers, was placed in a mortice in a large stone in the "Nauvoo House", and as the house was never finished, the water percolated through and dampened the papers so that they were not well preserved; and when the house was torn down the papers were taken by people who did not value them highly. Joseph F. afterwards obtained about a quire of the MS. in Oliver's hand writing, which he kindly showed to me. This part, though only a fragment of the book, may be useful as a test of my work. If my deductions are wrong, that MS. can be compared with our present edition, and if it is like it, it will do much toward settling my mind as to the truthfulness of Joseph Smith, for at present it looks like he has deceived us in the manner of translation and in accounting for the changes made in the second edition. I never investigated a matter which seemed to me more like a premeditated deception; and if I am mistaken I will heardly trust my mind to investigate anything again. I will do like thousands of others, let some one else do my thinking for me.

As evidence that the first edition was set according to copy, and that the present editions are wrong, we quote the following:

"In March, 1881, two gentlemen, named Kelley, residing in Michigan, for their own satisfaction, visited the neighborhood where Joseph spent his youth, and questioned the older residents who were acquainted with the Smith family as to their knowledge of the character of Joseph, his parents and his brothers and sisters. Their interviews with numerous parties who claim to have known Joseph were afterwards published. * * * * We here append a few extracts from these interviews. * * * *"

"What did you know about the Smiths, Mr. Gilbert?"

"I knew nothing myself; have seen Joseph Smith a few times, but not acquainted with him. Saw Hyrum quite often. I am the party that set the type from the original manuscript for the Book of Mormon. They translated it in a cave. I would know that manuscript to-day if I should see it. The most of it was in Oliver Cowdery's handwriting. Some in Joseph's wife's; a small part though. Hyrum Smith always brought the manuscript to the office; he would have it under his coat, and all buttoned up as carefully as though it was so much gold. He said at the time that it was translated from plates by the power of God, and they were very particular about it. We had a great deal of trouble

MAKING THE CHANGES. 109

with it. It was not punctuated at all. They did not know anything about punctuation, and we had to do that ourselves."

"Well; did you change any part of it when you were setting the type?"

"No, sir; we never changed it at all."

"Why did you not change it and correct it?

"Because they would not allow us to; they were very particular about that. We never changed it in the least. Oh, well; there might have been one or two words that I changed the spelling of; I believe I did change the spelling of one, and perhaps two, but no more."

"Did you set all the type, or did some one help you?"

"I did the whole of it myself, and helped to read the proof, too; there was no one who worked at that but myself. Did you ever see one of the first copies? I have one here that was never bound. Mr. Grandin, the printer, gave it to me. If you ever saw a Book of Mormon you will see that they changed it afterwards."

"They did! Well, let us see your copy; that is a good point. How is it changed now?"

"I will show you (bringing out his copy). Here on the title page it says (reading), 'Joseph Smith,

Jr., author and proprietor.' Afterwards, in getting out other editions they left that out, and only claimed that Joseph Smith translated it."

"Well, did they claim anything else than that he was the translator when they brought the manuscript to you?"

"Oh, no; they claimed that he was translating by means of some instruments he got at the same time he did the plates, and that the Lord helped him."

Myth of the M. F. page 58-9.

For the benefit of those who do not know, we explain that one Solomon Spaulding wrote a romance in the early part of this century, which he called, "The Manuscript Found," and many people believe it became the nucleus of the "Book of Mormon." "The Myth of the Manuscript Found" was written by Elder Reynolds for the purpose of proving that there was no connection between them. This quotation is made to prove that the Smith family was an honorable one. Our object in quoting it is to show that the printer followed copy as nearly as possible; making only such errors as passed unnoticed. That the publishers were very particular about it and would not allow it changed in the least. That Mr. Gilbert was struck with the fact that they would not allow him to correct the grammatical errors, and yet they afterwards corrected them themselves.

Elder Reynolds does not tell us where he gets the extract from, or I should endeavor to get the publication, for I believe there is more of it that would be of value here. It is hardly probable that two gentlemen who would say: "They did! Well, let us see your copy; that is a good point. How is it changed?", would be satisfied by being informed that the title page, that part of which was not translated from the plates at all was changed from "Joseph

Smith, Jr., author and proprietor," to "translated by Joseph Smith, Jun." I believe they followed with some such question as this: "What other changes have been made? Did they change the parts which they claimed had been translated by the Lord?" And of course the man who would say, "If you ever saw a 'Book of Mormon' you will see that they changed it afterwards." would be prepared to inform them by illustrating from all parts of the book.

A point of history connected with this quotation is that Mr. Gilbert says, the MS. was part in Oliver Cowdery's hand writing, and part in Joseph's wife's. If this is true, they must have taken the first copy to the printer and kept the second themselves. Joseph's mother, in her history, says Joseph went to Pennsylvania to see his wife, while Oliver copied the MS. "Whitney's History of Utah" says the same.

We wish now to call the reader's attention to the main reason for believing the errors in the first edition are not typographical. This one point alone we consider sufficient to convince any one able to read and think.

The corrections are just such as would be sure to have been made if the book had been written by a person who knew nothing of grammar, and afterwards learned a few of the simplest rules and then revise. For illustration look carefully through the changes on pages 42 to 47. Now turn to the illustrative extracts on pages 47 to 52. In these you can see the errors in the sentences. In the first we have "they which", changed to "those who", six times in one short verse, and "which", to "who", once besides. Again, we have "which", to "who", six times and "which", to "whom", twice in another short verse. In the next we have "which", to "who", six times, and in the next verse three times. "Which" is changed to who over seven hundred times in the book, and it is scattered all through, as will be seen by comparing the pages of changes. I think we are justified in saying that the clerk did not change his own manuscript so much from beginning to end; nor would the typo have set "which", in all these places if the copy had been written "who". And if he had done such a thing—but what is the use of speculating? No printer would make the same blunder so many times, from first to last of a large job like the Book of Mormon—but then if he had done such a thing, ever so poor a proof-reader would have discovered it before they had held copy on many forms. But if

MAKING THE CHANGES. 115

we will turn to the Bible we will see that the same mistake is there made; that is, the pronoun "which", is used in the Bible to refer to persons, which was good English when the Bible was translated, but it is not good English now, nor was it good in 1829.

It may be argued that since a change has taken place during the two hundred years, that Joseph may not have kept pace with the times, and a change of that kind could have been made a hundred years and the common people in the wilds of a new country, with the Bible continually before them would not have found it out. But we wish to keep it constantly before you, that Joseph had nothing to do with it, according to his own claims, and there is no excuse for God. He was not a backwoodsman. If that change was ever so new, God should have known it, and should have selected the proper pronoun. I have a New England geography printed in 1822, in which the pronoun "which" is used just as it is today. So until more light is thrown on the subject I shall believe that Joseph did not have any divine assistance in the translation of those wrong "whiches".

Now notice the double negatives on page 50. These sentences as they were in the first edition ment just the reverse of what they do in the present editions. The question is, did God operate the instrument so it produced the language of the first or the last.

When I noticed in I. Nephi 8:18, that Mary was said to be the mother of God Himself, I thought it must be a clerical error, but when I saw the same statement in the twenty-first verse, and again in the thirty-second, I saw no reason for laying such a blunder at the door of the poor printer. (Turn to page 51 and see how it has been amended by the addition of three words, "the son of.") Then when I read the following, I felt sure the printer had followed copy:

"1. And now Abinadi said unto them, I would that ye should understand that God himself shall come down among the children of men, and shall redeem his people;

2. And because he dwelleth in flesh, he shall be called the Son of God: and having subjected the flesh to the will of the Father, being the Father and the Son;

3. The Father, because he was conceived by the power of God; and the Son, because of the flesh; thus becoming the Father and Son:

4. And they are one God, yea, the very eternal Father of heaven and of earth;"

The above evidence is sufficient to convince me that the printer followed copy fairly well. There are a few real typographical errors in the first edition, but not many; I should judge that there are no more than we find in our well printed newspapers today. Yet Joseph F. told me personally that Grandin was a poor printer, and inferred that he was responsible for the bulk of the errors in the first edition.

There is another point of evidence that the errors are not typographical. This is a stronger point—if, indeed, it well could be—than the preceeding.

As the story goes, one, Lehi, with his family and some others, came from Jerusalem to America, 600 B. C. They brought with them a lot of brass plates containing the Old Testament scriptures up to that time. From these plates we have a few quotations, translated by the gift and power of God. So this part is not only better than the corresponding parts of the Bible, but it is absolutely perfect, if the eighth article of faith is anything to go by. So if we wish to see how nearly correct the Bible has been translated, a comparison of these parts would inform us. There are thirty-eight pages in the Book of Mormon which is also in the Bible. Six and one-half of these is the sermon on the mount, which Christ delivered in America almost exactly as he did in Jerusalem. The third and forth chapters of Malachi He quoted to them; making eight and one-half pages from the Son of God direct. The other twenty-nine and one half was taken from the brass plates by the various writers.

We wish now to call attention to the changes in these thirty-eight pages. Remember, Joseph translated them just as he did all the other parts of the book. Oliver copied it just as he did the balance of the book. The printer set it from the same hand writing. So it is plain that any errors which may have been made would not be any more likely to have any relation to the Bible than any other part of the book.

We find seventy-one changes in the thirty-eight pages, which is a falling off of over one third of the average of the book. Why should there be less typographical errors made in the work simply because the Bible contains the same matter. It looks still worse when we learn that the same errors that are common in the Bible are about the same, which reduces the changes, other than "which" to "who", to less than one-half the number found in the balance of the book. But the worst is still to come; eight are changes of spelling of proper names, so the number is cut down until there is not a

MAKING THE CHANGES. 121

grammatical blunder in all the changes of the thirty-eight pages, except as pointed out below.

The book of Mormon claims that many "plain and precious" parts have been taken out of the Bible. So of course we would expect to find some "plain and precious" parts added. Eight of the changes were made in the added parts, which leaves only sixty-three changes in the scripture proper. Sixty-three typographical errors! Sixty-three deviations from copy in the first edition. Would you now be surprised to learn that in forty-six of them the deviator selected the very word we have in King James' translation of the Bible? Yet this is a fact. Why should the printer, in deviating from copy, settle on the language of the Bible so much? Ah! No printer would do it. Joseph must have mistook a Bible for the plates on those several occasions. This is the only reasonable solution. But then he had to make some changes to account for the necessity of the translation. As might be expected, an illiterate person would be as likely to change one part as another; just as likely to take correct grammar and make it wrong as any other way. So we find thirteen of these changes from Bible language had to be brought back to avoid blunders. Eight out of the thirteen were grammatical errors, and two gave wrong meanings, while two were simply the change of the ancient to the modern style. But the other tells a big story to a printer. It is the change of "horner" to "homer". If the truth could be learned, I would bet all the old jack knives I had when I was a boy, that I can now find, against anything you have a mind to put up, that the Bible Joseph had behind curtain had a nicked "m", so it looked something like "rn". The word may have looked not very unlike "homer".

This leaves four out of sixty-three which was not like the Bible, first or last. Oh, how it resembles the work of a plagiarist! One of these is timely, it is the addition of the word "not", in Isaiah 2:9, first line, between, "boweth" and "down"; the urim and thummim having added another "not" between "himself" and "therefore". The verse agrees with my judgment better with the two additions; but remember God's translation only supplied one of them, the other being the work of the committee on revision.

I take it for granted that no one who has followed me will now say the blunders of the first edition are chargeable to the printer; but I fancy I hear the reader ask, "What of all these changes? They are trifling." I grant you they are small, but if Joseph had sat behind that curtain and seen that language come through the urim and thummim, he never would have changed it. Never! Here I fancy you may wonder whether Joseph made the bulk of the changes, or whether they were made by some subsequent revisor. To which we reply that a comparison of the first with the second edition shows ninety-five of the first hundred changed. So the first committee made about ninety-five per cent of the changes.

Now note the only deductions which can be made. Joseph, Oliver, Parley, John, and every other person who knowingly acquiesced in the revision, are all parties to a fraud. They are revising a book which has gone out with such claims of perfection that the only show is to say the copy was right as it came from the urim and thummim, but the printer blundered. And since, as we have abundantly proven, the printer did not make them, they "told the thing that was not", as Swift puts it. It is a plain case of wilful deception, to say the least. "What, you do not mean to say Joseph would lie about a thing of that kind do you?" Since he must have known the contents of the preface, I answer, yes. If he had cut Parley P. Pratt and John Goodson off the church for lying, as soon as the second edition was out we might have excused him. But had he done such a thing he would have been obliged to have given another reason for making near two thousand changes; and what reason could he have geven?

It might be asked if the first edition is not like the old language, with all its imperfections; and were not the changes allowable on that account? The only answer is no, because if this had been the case the revisors should have told us so in the preface, instead of telling us something else; unless, indeed, it can be shown beyond doubt that it has always been the policy of the church to "tell the thing that is not" and allow its subjects and the people in general to guess at the real truth.

There is one other reason why there are mistakes in the first edition, but it is rather against removing them for subsequent editions. It is as follows: "Condemn me not because of mine imperfections: neither my father because his imperfections; neither them that have written before him, but rather give thanks unto God that he hath made manifest unto you our imperfections, that ye may learn to be more wise than we have been." Mormon, 9:31.

Now we have it in its purity, after all this labor we finally learn that the errors were put there intentionally for a pedagogical effect. But what occasion have we to thank God, now that the errors are removed? For seven short years they had cause to be thankful, but how now? Oh, we have better schools. But since that time the church has passed through a period of almost no schools, and still they were deprived of that great amount of stimuli—the imperfections of the ancient mythical prophets of America. But such pedagogy does not agree with that of our modern teachers. They now say the teacher should never repeat an error in the hearing of the pupil, but on the contrary, the teacher should correct the pupil and get him to repeat his work corrected. But why should we set the judgment of the worldly wise up against God's prophets?

Now patient reader, if you have observed carefully the claims of the manner of translation, and noted the changes, and the reasons given for making them, I should like to ask, can you show me where I am wrong in concluding that the revising committee and all others who sanction such work are parties to a plain, premeditated prevarication?

We do not claim that this proves the Book of Mormon untrue, but we do think it goes a long way toward it. By showing that some the of claims are false, there is no dependence to be put in others. But we will hope to investigate further. If we find unimpeachable evidence in favor of the book we will be glad to believe it. But as I see it now, sufficient evidence could not be had to prove that Joseph and others did not practice deception wilfully.

www.ingramcontent.com/pod-product-compliance
Lightning Source LLC
Chambersburg PA
CBHW030403170426
43202CB00010B/1472